GROCERS
SELL US FOOD

Photo Credits:
© Chuck Keeler/Tony Stone Images: 4
© 1994 Gary Bublitz/Dembinsky Photo Assoc. Inc: cover
© 1997 Gary Bublitz/Dembinsky Photo Assoc. Inc: 6
© Gregg Andersen/Gallery 19: 3, 8, 10, 12, 14, 16, 18, 20, 22, 24, 26
© Jack McConnell: 28, 30

Library of Congress Cataloging-in-Publication Data

Greene, Carol.

Grocers sell us food/by Carol Greene.

p.   cm.

Summary: Describes, in simple text
and photographs, the jobs of the various
people who work in a grocery store.

ISBN 1-56766-561-6 (library reinforced : alk. paper)

1. Grocery trade—Juvenile literature.

2. Supermarkets—Juvenile literature.

3. Food industry and trade—Juvenile literature.

[1. Grocery trade. 2. Occupations.] I. Title.

HD9320.5.G73   1998   98-3100

381'.148—dc21   CIP

AC

GROCERS
SELL US FOOD

By Carol Greene

The Child's World®, Inc.

RATTLE! CLUNK!

Many people do different jobs in
this big supermarket.

CRINKLE! RUSTLE!

This young man puts people's food into bags. That is why he is called a **bagger**.

Sometimes baggers help people take food to their cars, too.

CLACKETY–CLACK! CLUNK!

Baggers also collect shopping carts from the parking lot. That's not much fun in bad weather!

CLICK! BEEP! BZZZZ!

The **checker** works at the front of the store. She passes each item over a screen.

BEEP!

A machine records the price.

RUSTLE! RUSTLE!

The checker takes the person's money. She puts it in a drawer.

CLINK! CLINK!

Then she gives the person change back. The **cash register** tells her how much change to give.

CLIP! SNIP! RUSTLE!

The **florist** works in the flower shop. She sells things such as plants, flowers, and seeds. She also has balloons and cards for people to buy.

THUD! THUD!

This man puts things on the shelves. He must make them look neat and tidy.

This worker straightens the fruits and vegetables. He checks to make sure they are fresh and clean, too.

"How may I help you?"

The workers at the service desk help people with problems. They also sell stamps and other things.

CHOP! CHOP!

The store's **butchers** know all about meat. They have had special training for their job.

BRRING!

The store manager has a huge job. He is in charge of all the other workers. He makes sure the building is in good shape.

Managing the store is hard work. Managers must know a lot of information. They must know about special sales in the store. They must be able to answer questions and help people, too.

With so much work to do, managers need lots of help—from the other workers!

This woman used to work in a supermarket. She started as a bagger. Now she and her husband own their own little grocery store.

They do all the jobs. That's just fine with them!

QUESTIONS AND ANSWERS

What do grocers do?

People who work in big supermarkets can do many different jobs. Some bag groceries. Some order stock. Others put stock on shelves. In small grocery stores, the same people do all these jobs and more. Most of all, though, grocers sell food to people who need it.

How do people learn to be grocers?

Many people start by working in a grocery store or supermarket. Some jobs—such as butcher—take special training. To become a manager, people must go to college and study business.

What kind of people are grocers?

People who run grocery stores should be good at business and math. They should also get along well with other people. They must know what people want to buy and how to display it well.

How much money do grocers make?

People who own grocery stores can make from $15,000 to $100,000 a year. People who work in stores make as much as $38,000 a year. But many make only the minimum wage.

GLOSSARY

bagger (BAG–ger)
A bagger is a person who puts groceries into bags for people to take home.

butcher (BU–tcher)
A butcher is someone who works in the meat department. Butchers see that all the meat is fresh and clean.

cash register (CASH REH-jih–ster)
A cash register is a machine that adds up money. A cash register also has a drawer that holds money.

checker (CHE–ker)
A checker is the person who collects people's money.

florist (FLO–rist)
A florist is someone who works with flowers and plants. Sometimes florists also sell balloons and cards.

INDEX

CAROL GREENE has published over 200 books for children. She also likes to read books, make teddy bears, work in her garden, and sing. Ms. Greene lives in Webster Groves, Missouri.